UNCOMFORTABLE

"There Will Be No Change Without Discomfort"

UNCOMFORTABLE

"There Will Be No Change Without Discomfort"

JESSICA SELVY-DAVIS

ISBN: 978-0692141922

ACKNOWLEDGEMENTS

This work would not have been possible without the inspiration of Holy Spirit. I am especially grateful for my husband Apostle Jonathan Davis and son Jacqavious, who have been supportive of my ministry as a scribe and have worked actively to provide me with prayer and time to effectively release this message to the masses. I am also grateful to all of those who worked diligently to assist with the production and promotion of this book. I want to thank God for my Pastors, George W. Stewart and Jacqueline W. Stewart, who have provided to me extensive spiritual guidance and taught me a great deal about my creative gift. As my teacher and mentor, Pastor George W. Stewart has taught me more than I could ever give him credit for here. He has shown me, by his example, what a creative vessel should be.

Nobody has been more important to me in the pursuit of this book than the members of my family. I would like to thank my parents, Jesse and Johnnie Selvy, for being the ultimate role models. I'd also like to thank my brothers, sisters, nieces, and nephews whose love and strength are with me in whatever I pursue. Most importantly, I wish to thank my loving and supportive Kingdom Seekers family who provide unending inspiration and motivation as I seek to glorify God with my gift of writing.

Special thanks to One Shot Media Solutions, Jekalyn Carr, Ashley Sutton, Lady Tina Carter, Latasha Snow, Laquita Selvy and Danielle "Qwiet Storm" Glenn for your joint supply in authoring this book. I greatly appreciate each of you!

TABLE OF CONTENTS

FOREWORD

Jessica Davis has done it once more! This highly acclaimed, inspiring book will impart knowledge of how people should change their perspective on how they look at God's divine purpose and destiny for their lives. God strategically places his people in various situations in their lives to grow. This book implies that every place you end up in may not feel pleasant. However, when you learn to value your discomfort, you will rise higher, accomplish more, and live your best life.

After reading this remarkable book, you will be equipped for the extraordinary plans of God that will cause you to prosper! With that being said, "THANK YOU" Pastor Jessica for obeying the voice of God and releasing this amazing tool to help individuals expand in their God purposed lives.

-Jekalyn Carr

INTRODUCTION

Change and growth is proceeded by discomfort. While it may not feel like it in the moment, a little bit of discomfort goes a long way in terms of personal development. Sure. No one likes feeling uncomfortable, but it's a big part of improving your progress.

Routines may make you feel at ease and in control, but what a constant routine really does is dull your sensitivity. Think about the times in your life when you've driven the same route repeatedly. After a certain number of trips, you start tuning out most of it. Have you ever done something and didn't remember what happened after you did it? If you don't get out of your comfort zone, you might find yourself just existing and not living or simply just doing enough to get by and never going beyond your capabilities.

When you go out of your way to experience new things or when you let new things happen to you, your body creates brand new neural pathways that fuel your creative spark and enhance your memory. In one study, researchers tested the memory of participants by showing them images which were rated as novel, familiar and very familiar. The best results came when people were shown a novel image followed by a familiar one. *(Public Library of Science)* So, while repetition helps with memory, mixing in new information is important as well. That's why being uncomfortable is something you should embrace.

God puts us in new and unfamiliar situations to trigger perpetual change and growth as believers. Few people actually enjoy the feeling of being uncomfortable. The challenge is to get past that initial feeling of wanting to return to the norm so that you can grow and benefit from that discomfort.

Although not all discomfort serves a positive purpose or will contribute to your growth, we must be selective about how, when, and why we're embracing the discomfort of a given situation. We also choose to see how it can benefit us as we navigate through life. Ultimately, you have to find the courage, awareness, and understanding that allows you to see problems and hurdles for what they really are. They are opportunities to change and grow into the person God created you to be!

CHAPTER ONE

"Get Comfortable Being Uncomfortable"

"Get Comfortable Being Uncomfortable" is a U.S. Navy SEALs motto that simply means that if you can be comfortable being uncomfortable, you'll be equipped to handle any kind of situation or circumstance that you face in life. This not only applies to the extreme physical conditions they endure, but also to the situations they endure during their rigorous training. Upon extensive research, I found that US Navy SEALs go through what's called surf torture, a process where everyone links arms and lies down in the frigid ocean until the body reaches early stages of hypothermia. They do this daily before taking on whatever other tasks are required of them. This process teaches them to stay focused on what they need to accomplish despite how uncomfortable they feel.

Did you know that God will allow situations and circumstances in your life to make you feel uncomfortable? Truth is, you will never change, leave, go, move, stop, or mature until God turns over your nest. This harsh feeling is not to hurt you, but to help push you out of your comfort zone. So, if you've been feeling uncomfortable lately, it just means that it's time to undergo evolutionary change.

In Psalm 119:71 the Psalmist says, *"It is good for me that I have been afflicted (Made Uncomfortable) that I might learn thy statutes."* Here, the psalmist is acknowledging that he needed the discipline of the Lord in his life and this discipline came to him in the context of feeling uncomfortable.

In this passage, the affliction isn't specified. The affliction could have been the persecution of the unbelievers that he mentions in verses 69 and 70, or it could have been a more active affliction by the Lord of him, or it could have been both and more. Throughout the Psalm he acknowledges that this discipline was one of the ways that the Lord dealt well and wisely with him. Twice he says, "The Lord humbled me." In verses 67 and 71, "I went astray, but now I keep your word...'I was afflicted (*Made Uncomfortable*) that I might learn your statutes." So in both of those instances, the affliction that he experienced humbled him and actually set him on the way of the Lord. Although he doesn't tell us what the form of discomfort was, it could have been physical suffering, emotional anguish, or even the mental suffering of the lies and the insensitivity of the unbelievers who were mentioned in verses 69 and 70. Whatever the form was, he became comfortable being uncomfortable by accepting it from God as divine discipline, acknowledging that it was wise and effective.

Is this your confession when you experience discomfort or do you murmur and complain that God does not understand what He is doing? So often the latter response is the case. We think we know better than God because we have not learned the important lessons of why He makes us uncomfortable once we've finally arrived to a place of comfort. Well, believe it or not, there are some valuable lessons that we can learn from being uncomfortable.

One lesson we can learn from being uncomfortable is that it's not about us, but about God. When God makes us uncomfortable, it is to draw our attention to the fact that HE is in control of our lives. This feeling is meant to draw our attention to God and this fact alone is worth every uncomfortable feeling that He sends our way. So often we go through life with little thought of God and what His will is for our lives. Discomfort has a way of bringing life to a screeching halt and leading us to see that we are finite human beings and God is the infinite, almighty and all-knowing God. That is why the Psalmist said it was good to have been afflicted. It drove him back to God and His statutes. Similarly, feeling uncomfortable should drive us back to God and His Word. As we do so, we will learn that God is not afflicting us arbitrarily, but He is doing so as our Heavenly Father and that He might do us good at our latter end *(Deut. 8:5,16)*.

Another lesson we can learn from the feeling of discomfort is that God is more concerned about our salvation and sanctification than He is concerned about our usefulness in any particular area of life. That is a staggering thought! When sickness sets in, unemployment hits, or natural disasters strike, our lives can be rendered seemingly useless in a moment. Our first thought is, "What am I going to do now?" But have you ever considered this thought, "What is God telling me now? How am I going to be changed and grow through this? How will I be even more fit for glory?" Such a mindsets give a different perspective when we are faced with uncomfortable situations and circumstances – it gives a certain

10

element of sweetness to know that Christ is being formed in us, rather than our own wretched sinful nature being perpetuated.

Again, being uncomfortable can draw out what is in our own hearts. Remember, afflictions are sent to show us where we are as well as tell others if our trust is in God or ourselves.

Your feelings of discomfort can be used or abused. When they are used correctly, you will use them to witness to others about the goodness of God. When you abuse them, you will complain and murmur against God for dealing you another blow. What is in your heart? Have you became comfortable being uncomfortable? Can you say that it was good that you were afflicted because it brought you to reckon with God again? Can you say it was good that you were afflicted because it brought you to trust in Christ for the first time or afresh? Can you say it was good that you were afflicted because it taught you to glorify God and be a witness of the goodness of God to others? If so, you are changing for the better and growing into a greater you!

CHAPTER TWO

"Pruning & Provoking: We're NOT Entitled to a Comfortable Life!"

This may be a hard pill to swallow but buckle down and take it...... "YOU'RE NOT ENTITLED TO A LIFE OF COMFORT AND EASE!" Yes, you heard me right. We are not entitled to that life. No matter what our culture teaches us, or what the media portrays, life in Christ is not supposed to be stuck and stagnant. God never said that would be our reality. Truth is, He is always pruning and provoking his people to do more, grow more, learn more, and serve more.

Discomfort is the perfect tool for pruning and provoking us. It's God's way of removing the unwanted "branches" in our lives without harming us. He refers to us as trees and we all sometimes need pruning and provoking in our spiritual life. Jesus Christ reminds us of this when He says, *"I am the true vine, and My Father is the vinedresser. Every branch in Me that does not bear fruit He takes away; and every branch that bears fruit He prunes, that it may bear more fruit" (John 15:1-2).*

Being pruned and provoked is very uncomfortable because it involves cutting off superfluous branches, those things in us that hinder us from truly being better, doing better, looking better and feeling better. Our Father knows the beauty that He hopes we can become when He says, *"For I know the thoughts that I think toward you, says the LORD, thoughts of peace and not of evil, to give you a future and a hope" (Jeremiah 29:11).* God envisions us becoming part of His family. When He prunes us, He has that vision in mind. So go ahead and get comfortable being uncomfortable so that you can flourish and live a beautiful life for His glory.

Sorry; God does not agonize over pruning and provoking us because He knows that it will help us, not harm us. Our discomfort, whether natural or spiritual, doesn't seem pleasant, but it really is necessary for change and growth. Be careful as you walk through seasons of discomfort, pain and uneasiness that the devil doesn't push you into being frustrated with God when it seems like He is so far away or like He is ignoring your prayers. Sometimes the feeling of being alone with a pile of unanswered prayers while constantly asking God to make things easier causes us to lose sight of the fact that being uncomfortable is meant to CHALLENGE US TO CHANGE. Instead of asking Him to make it easier, we should ask Him for the grace and endurance to grow through it!

Furthermore, who are we to ask God to change His mind? We have no idea what He has in store. We can't even imagine how He is going to use our discomfort to impact the world! If He took this cup from you, would His impact on the world through you be the same? When I think about it like this, it almost feels selfish to not want God to prune and provoke me to change. Let me assure you that if you allow Him, God will use your situation to impact the world and your testimony to grow His Kingdom!

Don't be discouraged! Sometimes pruning and provoking does involve trials. We must remember Hebrews 12:5-6, which says *"Do not despise the chastening of the LORD, nor be discouraged when you are rebuked by Him; for whom the LORD loves He chastens."* Adam Clarke's Commentary on the Bible says the following about these verses: "Here is the reason why we should neither neglect correction, nor faint under it: It is a proof of the fatherly love of God Almighty, and shows his most gracious designs towards us; from which we may be fully convinced that the affliction will prove the means of good to our souls, if we make a proper use of it."

Barnes' commentary on verse 10 follows with a similar thought: "This is the elevated object at which God aims by our trials. It is not that he delights to produce pain; not that he envies us and would rob us of our little comforts... it is, that he may make us more pure and holy, and thus promote our own best interest." Remember, God is pruning and provoking you to become like Him so he does not have a problem disrupting your life of comfort!

CHAPTER THREE

"Good Is Good, But Greater Is Better"

In Ecclesiastes 7:8a, King David's beloved son, Solomon, the man of wisdom, made this profound statement, *"Better is the end of a thing than the beginning thereof."* Good is good, but greater is always a better outcome! Often when we look at where we are in our lives or what we have accomplished, we see ourselves as being pretty good people and have done some pretty good things as well. However, if we just stop and settle for good, we will never know that greater feels much better.

What does the scripture say? God's Word defines what our outlook should be toward all that God has called us to experience by His grace. Ecclesiastes 3:11b says, *"...no man can find out the work that God maketh from the beginning to the end."* We are very limited in our understanding of what God is doing in our lives. The end is better for God's people because the Lord is very much interested in change and growth. God's thinking is never "good is good enough."

We are evolving every day and the Lord is saying to us, in the b part of Ecclesiastes 7:8, that we are in need of patience in the process. We see this same principle in Romans 5:3 that tribulation (*Discomfort*) is to work patience into our lives. It's no less than the fructifying work of the Spirit in our lives in Galatians 5:22 that God is interested in. Hebrews 10:35-36 admonishes us not to cast away our confidence, but to plug patience into the equation as we wait to receive the fulfillment of God's promises towards us. There is always so much more that God wants to do in us and through us for his glory. We will never see that greater is a better place if we get stuck in a good place.

Consider Job's life. Job 8:7 says, *"Though thy beginning was small, yet thy latter end should greatly increase."* How true this was for God's servant, Job. In Job 42:1-2 the double portion that Job received at the end of his trial. How true this was for Ruth, as Love lifted her out of an incestuous line into the royal line of King David from which Christ came. How true this was for Esther, who was prepared by the Holy Spirit in a place of obscurity

14

for her moment in history. How true this was for the woman with the issue of blood, as Jesus gifted her with a divine healing and her faith in Christ opened a new door for her into His peace. How true this will be for you and I, our Father's children, who are all glorious within!

Live with divine patience in the process and God may even give insight into how the end of your situation is better. Are you concerned over your failures? Through confession and rebound *(1 John 1:9)* and receiving God's grace, you will get to know the God of all Grace towards you and the end will be better. The end of chastisement is better when it results in peaceable fruits of righteousness *(Hebrews 12:11)*. The end of suffering is better as those who suffer with Him will reign with Him in 2 Timothy 2:11-13. Through the mind of Christ, we can form correct judgments regarding all of life experiences, and his loving kindness toward us will be better than all we experience. *(Psalm 63:3)*. Hear counsel and receive instruction [on this matter], and you will be wise in the latter end *(Proverbs 19:20)*. It's time for a sustainable leap from doing and being good to being and doing greater!

POINTS TO PONDER:

•It's good that you and your mate can go on a date, but IT'S GREAT when you can date and communicate.

•It's good that you have enough for yourself, but IT'S GREAT to have more than you need to share with others.

•Your life is good now that you're saved, but it becomes GREAT when you live it healed, delivered and restored.

•It's good that you have a house, car, job, family and friends, but IT'S GREAT to have it all with peace.

•It's good to have treasures on earth, but wouldn't it be GREAT to have treasures laid up in heaven?

You must care about your greater so much that you're willing to let go of lesser at the drop of a dime? If so, start by giving up some things, changing the way you see some things, shifting how you do some things, and then open up and allow God to teach you how to embrace greater things. Go ahead and get familiar with overcoming hurdles that make you fear being uncomfortable because this is God's way of getting you to all of what He has in store for you!

CHAPTER FOUR

"Push Yourself Past Your Comfort Zone"

At some point, you are going to say to yourself, "I've never done this before" or "I don't know what I'm doing." We've all been there and here's a biblical principle: Don't say it out loud! Faith it till you make it. It's scary, but I promise you this: When it's over, you are going to say, "It wasn't as bad as I thought it was." Fear kills more dreams than failure ever will.

QUESTION:
- Do you recognize your comfort zones? Are you set in your ways?
- Considering your personality, are you basically flexible or inflexible?
- How do you view life at this moment?
- What would it take to break you out of your comfort zone?

The comfort zone, as defined by Lifehacker, is a "behavioral space where your activities and behaviors fit a routine and pattern that minimizes stress and risk." The operative words here being stress and risk. In our comfort zone there is a sense of familiarity, security and certainty. When we step outside of our comfort zone, we're taking a risk and opening ourselves up to the possibility of stress and anxiety; we're not quite sure what will happen and how we'll react.

Let me assure you that the only thing that is secure in life is God and He has given you the ability to contribute at a greater level to something or someone that matters to you in life. When you live from that knowledge and experience, you'll find (and create) gainful, rewarding opportunities to grow despite the turbulence around you. To do that, you must continually push yourself out of your comfort zone.
The people who do this successfully are able to make a tremendously positive impact and find even more opportunities to make a difference. It is possible to be successful maintaining the status quo, but true differentiation is achievable only for those who are willing to dive into the unfamiliar.

17

Staying in your comfort zone can result in consistent, steadyperformance, but stepping out of your comfort zone into a new and challenging level can create the conditions for greater results. Margie Warrell said it best, "In an increasingly competitive, cautious and accelerated world, those who are willing to take risks, step out of their comfort zone and into the discomfort of uncertainty will be those who will reap the biggest rewards."

Clearly, comfort is doing what everyone else does – conforming to norms and to the pressure around you. By pushing yourself into new areas, you will have a chance to authentically define who you are and break free of the limitations of what others think you should be.

We struggle to step outside of our comfort zones because we are wired to seek out comfort, which makes it hard to let it go. However, doing so is an important and almost universal factor in personal growth. How can we expect to evolve in our lives naturally and spiritually if we only stick to habit and routine? As children, we're natural risk-takers and we quickly find out that reaching new heights involves the risk of attempting something we might not succeed at right away. As a result, we grow up fearing failure which prevents us from attempting new things. This comes at a high cost to our tremendous potential for lifelong growth and transformation.

Those of us who've been forced to change understand that what is comforting is often not what is best for you. Leaving your comfort zone can create a tremendous feeling of confidence and self-respect as you learn what you are truly capable of doing and creating, which is far greater and more expansive than you ever dreamed. Pushing past your limits helps you find the fulfillment, excitement, and meaning you have been searching for in all the wrong places.

Here are a few principles from Pauls' experience in *Matthew 14:22-32* that can help you push past your comfort zone:

1. **FACE YOUR FEARS**
   - Peter left the known to discover the knowable.
   - Peter had to deal with his fear to get out of the boat. He'd never seen anyone walk on water!
   - Peter thought, "If Jesus can do it, by His power so can I." He understood something about being in fellowship with Jesus.
   - Peter had confidence in His Lord.
   - He makes a request.
   - He demonstrates trust and dependence on the Lord's power and authority.
   - He dared to do the impossible and stepped out in faith.

2. **YOU MUST LEARN TO FOCUS ON JESUS**
   - What dominates your focus?
   - In the midst of the process don't focus on the feelings of discomfort.
   - You can't be unwilling to refocus on Jesus once you've stepped out.

3. **YOU MUST BE WILLING TO MAKE MISTAKES.**
   - Jesus saw him as a potential leader. He saw a man who didn't wear masks, a man who could trust and move beyond what was comfortable.
   - You must be willing to take risks even if you make mistakes.
   - Don't get stuck on a mistake as if you're not able to move beyond it.

4. **CHALLENGE YOUR COMFORT ZONE**
   - Identify your comfort zone.
   - Recognize God is at work.
   - Ask Him to reveal what He is doing in your life.
   - Repent for wanting to stay comfortable where you are.
   - Find you an accountability partner who refuses to allow you to settle for being comfortable with where you are.

If you never leave your comfort zone you are likely sabotaging your chances for lasting success and happiness. Don't be afraid to try something new in any aspect of your life. You will find you are more resilient, capable and courageous than you once believed, and as you rise to these challenges, more exciting ones are awaiting.

Ask yourself, "When was the last time I really wanted to try something, but I shied away?" Next time you find yourself hesitating, go for it. Taking risks and believing in yourself allows you to be a better person and a greater blessing to others. Your testimony will be that the reward (and the lessons learned) were without question, worth the risk!

CHAPTER FIVE

"Man, I Forgot the Milk"

I told myself, "Okay, mental note: I have got to make cornbread for dinner and I need to get milk from the grocery store." Then the next thing I know, I'm pouring in all my ingredients and look in the fridge and realize "Man, I forgot to get milk." Now the local market is closed, Walmart is too far and dinner is almost done. I am in an uncomfortable spot right now and don't know what to do. Do I panic? Do I pout? Do I throw the whole bowl away? Do I borrow a cup from the neighbor or do I do what I've never done? I didn't have time to ponder long, so I had to rely on God for instructions. My discomfort lead me to discover that Hot Water made the best Cornbread cakes. Can you believe that my Mistake on the plate with Collard Greens, Yams, Mac and Cheese, and Fried Chicken Oooooowee turned out to be the new family favorite?

To see the smile on my family's face helped me realize that it is possible for a miracle to come out of a mistake! Forgetting the milk was indeed a simple mistake, but the miracle of hot water cornbread was a blessing I definitely wasn't expecting. As humans, we all make mistakes. We goof up and create mess. We mishear, misinterpret, misjudge, misread, misspeak, misspell, misunderstand, and yes, make the mistake of forgetting the main thing, *Romans 8:28 "And we know that all things work together for good to those who love God, to those who are the called according to His purpose."* Let me encourage you by saying that there is no mistake you make can ever be too great to cancel out God's plan for your life. No matter what you've done, if you will shake off the frustrations of being uncomfortable and move forward in your thinking and expectations, God will get you to where you're supposed to be and get to you what you're supposed to have. Regardless of how uncomfortable it feels, just trust God. He is prepared to take your mistake, your awful circumstance, and turn it into a miracle!

I admonish you to not let the fear of making mistakes prevent you from trying anything new or moving out of your comfort zone. Just the word "mistake" will strike fear in your minds when it really shouldn't because this is not the will of God for your life! Mistakes are not always bad, especially when they initiate greater growth. You must focus on what you learned from the mistake and how to improve from it. Be who you are. Trust in yourself. It will come back to you in amazing ways. Don't be so focused on achieving one particular outcome that you miss all kinds of wonderful opportunities because you fear making mistakes. It's not worth wasting your time agonizing over things in the past because you can't change what happened. Just recognize that you simply made a mistake and keep pressing forward to the future. After all, you're not a failure because you made a mistake. You and the mistake are not the same thing at all. Take the time to learn something valuable from it and focus on a solution that prevents you from making the same mistake again.

A great example of how God can work in a miraculous way after making a mistake is the story of Joseph in Genesis 37-47. Joseph had an awesome dream, but made a huge mistake by sharing it with his brothers. They hated him and threw him into a pit. They sold him as a slave and he was taken to a foreign country. People lied on him and as a result, he was thrown into prison. Joseph encountered a lot of uncomfortable situations, but God took care of him through it all. The Lord took all of the tragedies of Joseph's mistake and turned them into a fantastic miracle that not only blessed Joseph, but ended up saving the lives of his family and countless others in the land of Egypt and throughout the known world. God has not changed. He can do the same thing for you. Regardless of the discomfort you're in, with God on your side, you can't lose. Again, Apostle Paul assured us of this in Romans 8:28, *"And we know that all things work together for good to those who love God, to those who are the called according to His purpose."* All things includes your mistakes, your failures, and even the attacks of the devil. If you'll pray, if you'll love God and endeavor to do what He wants you to do, if you'll walk in His purposes, He can and will turn things around for you.

Let God Use Your Mistakes

Without God, our mistakes would still be mistakes, but with God, our mistakes are made new, and we get to write a whole new ending. Before we let God use our mistakes for the good, we need to first admit and confess our sins to Him. Proverbs 28:13-14 tells us that, *"Whoever tries to hide his sins will not succeed, but the one who confesses his sins and leaves them behind will find mercy."* Once we know we are forgiven of our mistakes, we have to trust that God will use them in some capacity for His glory. Give God the opportunity to redeem your mistakes, just as He redeemed Joseph and his brothers.

You say, "Okay, I believe God can change things for me, but why should He? Why would God do that?" Deuteronomy 23:5 tells us why! *The Lord your God turned the curse into a blessing for you, because the LORD your God loves you.* God loves you and He cares for you too, that's why He is willing to turn your mistake into the greatest miracle in your life. Yes, God loves you! So no matter what you're going through today, give it over to God. When you do, watch what He does to work every uncomfortable situation out for your good!

PRAY: Dear Lord, I am calling upon You today for Your divine help. I am in an uncomfortable place and need a supporting hand to keep me on the right and just path. It doesn't feel good right now but Lord, I reach out to You for Your guidance. Please show me which way to turn. Calm my anxious thoughts, come speak into my mind. Strengthen me as I falter and feel weary. I trust that You are with me and know what's best for me always. Amen!

CHAPTER SIX

"Man, I Forgot The Milk Again!"

Have you ever gone to Walmart or your local grocery store to get a few essential items like milk, eggs, bread & etc., but got distracted by so many other things that were on sale that you really didn't need. You finally make it to the counter with a basket full of unintended items, check out, load the car, and head home. While putting away your haul, you discover, "I forgot the milk, again." You now have a lot of good things, but didn't remember to get the main thing.

To remember is important and I've learned that making a To Do List helps me remember not to forget what's most important. It's so easy to get caught up in the everyday hustle and bustle of life that we make the mistake of forgetting our God-given purpose. It's very possible to do everything except what we've been predestined to do. This is how we can have everything we want, but still need so much! We get distracted with "Living life like it's golden" and forget that living life with purpose is the main thing. Before we came here, God and Jesus Christ created an earthly home where we could stretch out our wings to fulfill our potential. He knew we would face pain and hardship, but He also knew that without it we wouldn't grow.

Being able to put our lives in context of where we came from brings clarity as we establish priorities and make choices during our lives here on earth. We begin to understand God's unique point of view as we consider that each life on earth is unique and each one of us will experience discomfort differently. Some discomfort include physical challenges, but all involve temptations and difficulties of one kind or another. We each have specific strengths and weaknesses and our Father knows us well. He knows how we can effectively grow from our experiences and He gives us commandments to enable us to reach our potential, but it's up to us whether we will choose to obey. It is our choice to help, hinder, learn or leave things undone. It is our choice to prove that we can become more like Him. When we have a better understanding why we are here and what we are working to achieve, we can make choices that will make our Heavenly Father proud, make our lives more purposeful, and ultimately, help us become more like Him. Just as we have to-do lists to help us manage every area of our lives naturally, I believe that a to-do list can help us come to understand His purpose for us. We become more responsible for our choices spiritually.

The benefits of creating to-do list are that we remember to prioritize our time and they give us a clear vision of what we should be doing now. I want to challenge you to create a strategic plan for remembering what you've been purposed to do in life and the accomplishments you want to be proud of as you grow. Yes, your very own Spiritual To Do List! This kind of list can help you stay focused and moving forward as you push past discomfort to discover the greatness that hasn't yet been revealed in you. It's a very simple strategy that works great!

MY "TO DO LIST" (Fill In Blank)

1. I will not stop _____.

2. I will finish _____.

3. I will graduate with _____.

4. I will pursue _____.

5. I plan to _____ by the age of _____.

6. I will start _____.

7. My purpose is _____and I will use it to _____.

8. I will read at-least _____ scriptures a day.

9. I will commit to praying for myself and others for _____ a day.

10. I am letting go of _____ to embrace_____.

11. I am a better _____, _____, _____ and _____.

12. My top 3 goals are to

*   _____
    _____

*   _____
    _____

*   _____
    _____

CONFESSION: I walk by faith and not by fear because I believe God's Word. I expect the very best and I expect to succeed and not fail. I am pressing forward and not backwards because I'm expecting my future to work out perfectly. According to my earnest expectation and hope, this situation of discomfort I am in right now I receive as God's will for my life and I will not refute it. I believe and I receive the manifestation of my confessions right now! In Jesus's name, Amen!

CHAPTER SEVEN

"No More Nesting"

Deuteronomy 32:11, 12 (NKJV)
"As an eagle stirs up its nest, hovers over its young, spreading out its wings, taking them up, carrying them on its wings, so the LORD alone led him, and there was no foreign god with him."

As I studied the significance of "The Eagle's Nest," I learned a very valuable lesson about our own relationship with God. Eagles are truly one of the most remarkable creatures God created. According to Wikipedia, the nest of the eagle is built high upon the mountain ranges. They will at times decide on a location that can reach altitudes of 10,000 feet. The nesting eagles will build a nest that can reach a weight of up to two tons and stretch to as much as eight feet across. They have the wearisome task of carrying limbs up to four inches in diameter to the nesting area. The nest can be as deep as two feet. The core of the nest is supported by the huge limbs and the outer edges of the nest are then lined with soft leaves and vines that are actually woven together by the eagles before the laying of the eggs. The leaves cover the rough sticks that would puncture the soft fur of the eaglets. In addition to the soft bed of leaves, shortly before the eggs hatch, the mother eagle begins to pull the soft downy fur from her own body to shelter and warm her young.

After about six to seven months, the mother eagle swoops in one day and begins to stir or basically wreck the brooding area of the nest. She pulls out the soft leaves, tosses the rabbit fur to the winds, and removes the long vines that once provided comfort to them. It then becomes a task for the eaglets to stand and balance themselves in the nest that has been stirred. The alternative is not an option, because to lie down would cause lacerations from the limbs in the nest. The mother eagle teaches her little ones to fly by making their nest so uncomfortable that they are forced to leave it and commit themselves to the unknown world of air outside. She knows that an eagle learns to fly through struggle and God knows that the transformation we need from being a helpless, baby bird in a comfortable nest to becoming a majestic eagle soaring through the sky does not come about by accident. In fact, it is a very painful and uncomfortable process.

In verse 11, Moses describes two mysterious things the mother eagle does to prepare her young eaglets for flight.

FIRST, THE EAGLE STIRS UP ITS NEST

Again, when the mother eagle "stirs up the nest" she removes all the rabbit's fur, lamb's wool and the soft leaves she used to construct her nest so that all that's left are the prickly sticks and briars. So picture this: One day that nest is all soft and cozy, but the next day it becomes a bed of discomfort and restlessness. Those little eaglets are no longer comfortable. That is exactly the way "Mama Eagle" wants it. Sure it breaks the heart of that mama eagle to listen to her young eaglets "whining and complaining" about how uncomfortable they are, but in her wisdom, the mama eagle knows what is best for her children. She knows if she doesn't "stir up the nest" and allow her eaglets to experience discomfort they will never leave the nest to become the beautiful, majestic birds God created them to be.

SECOND, THE STRUGGLE OF THE FLIGHT

This part of the process is even more painful because the mother eagle "hovers over her young" refusing to feed them any longer. Instead of going out to get food to bring back to them, she settles down in the nest with her wings spread over them to protect them. At first this may seem very cruel and unfair, but the mother eagle knows that in order for her young eaglets to mature and be able to survive on their own, she has to create a hunger within them to leave the nest and go out and hunt for themselves.

THIRD, CARRYING HER YOUNG ON HER WINGS

Researchers who have studied the nature of eagles describe this as a frightening, yet fascinating thing to behold. The mother eagle will mount the young eaglet on her wings, leave the nest then soar thousands of feet into the air. When she gets to a certain altitude, the mother eagle will flap her wings causing that eaglet to go into a "free fall." As that eaglet tumbles downward, it will start flapping its wings trying to learn how to fly. And just when it looks like the young eaglet is going to crash to the earth below, the mother eagle will swoop down and catch her young eaglet on her back and start climbing back into the sky again. Can you imagine that little eaglet with eyes as big as planet earth crying, "Mama, what are you trying to do? Don't you love me?" Mama's silence is deafening! When she reaches a certain altitude she flaps her wings and once again, her young eaglet goes into a free fall. This painful process is repeated until the eaglet learns to fly. Just as a mother eagle allows her young eaglets to struggle, GOD ALLOWS HIS PEOPLE TO STRUGGLE!

Remember when Moses sent the twelve spies to spy out the Promised Land and bring back a report of what they had found? Remember ten of the twelve spies brought back "a bad report" about the giants they saw and all of the terrible things that would happen to the Israelites if they tried to enter the Promised Land? Despite Joshua and Caleb's "good report" and their challenge to "take the land" God had promised to them, the Israelites believed the "bad report." The eaglets weren't ready to fly, so in order to increase their faith and trust, God had to "stir up the nest." He did that by putting the Israelites in a desolate, uncomfortable wilderness where they would have to depend upon Him for everything for forty long years.

The nest is our "comfort zone," our place of familiarity and herein lies the problem! The longer we stay in the nest of our comfort zone, the less our faith and trust in God grows. In fact, we become complacent, indifferent and we start stagnating spiritually. If it were left up to you and I, we would stay in the nest of comfort the rest of our lives and never venture out by faith. This is why God in His infinite wisdom stirs up the nest. That job folds, the relationship stops working, alcohol and drugs stop working. There's a change in supervisors at work, teachers at school, friends, or it may mean getting new areas of responsibility handed to you in ministry. Truth is, God may stir up the nest in a number of ways, and though it is painful and unpleasant, we must have enough faith and trust in God to believe He is doing it for our own good.

How you and I respond to the discomforts of life makes all the difference in the world.

- If you give up or quit, you'll never learn to fly by faith.
- If you feel sorry for yourself and throw "pity parties" you'll never learn to fly by faith.
- If you go around telling everybody your "woe is me" stories, you'll never learn to fly by faith.
- If you shut yourself up in your house and pull the covers over your head, you'll never learn to fly by faith.

If you will start "flapping your wings of faith" and trust in the Lord with all your heart and lean not on your own understanding, He will help you to "soar like an eagle."

What trials are you going through right now? Instead of looking at your trials as burdensome, look at them as God's way of "stirring up the nest" so you will grow, mature and "take flight" to new levels of faith you've never been to before.

CONFESSION: God is pushing me out of the nest and teaching me how to fly and I Thank Him!

CHAPTER EIGHT

"Who Told You Different Was Bad?"

Becoming aware that you must do things differently is the first step toward positive change and growth. It's the first step toward solving the problem, or getting the need met; the first step toward the future. It's how we focus on the next lesson.

Discomfort gets our attention and prepares us for change. The process of becoming changed begins with being uncomfortable.

THIS IS THE FORMULA:
Uncomfortable + Awareness + Acceptance = Change

Truth is, when feeling "UNCOMFORTABLE" *(causing or feeling unease or awkwardness)* you must ACCEPT *(believe or come to recognize)* the temporary discomfort from AWARENESS *(knowledge or perception of a situation or fact)* if you expect to see CHANGE *(to become different)*.

We all have different life experiences and they are greatly influenced by the environment in which we are raised. We're more familiar with certain people, places and views that we're exposed to. The older we get and the more we define the world around us based on each of our unique experiences, the less open we are to different possibilities. Most people were specifically trained to avoid what we label as "bad" and only seek what our mind labels as "good." The problem with this is that as we grow, the routine labeling that we do in relation to our lives grows stronger and more permanent within us. This process goes on until we get to a point where we really understand that different isn't bad at all. Our habit of avoiding the bad, seeking the good, and not inviting uncertainty and risk, essentially lives our lives for us. Through our being trained to label discomfort as negative, we've completely written off the ability to grow through difficult times. Our ordinary response to difficult situations is to avoid them, numb ourselves from actually feeling the reality of life, and blaming the entire world instead of choosing to do things differently. Being truthful about who we are and where we are allows us the room we need to grow. Allow me to share a few practical steps you can take to get there.

Step One: Recognizing growth opportunities

Most of us get to a point in our lives where we accept the person we've become. "I don't do public speaking." "I'm not a good dancer." "Marriage isn't for me." "I don't really enjoy church." "I'm not a people person." These are just a few boundaries we have set on ourselves. Beyond the qualities and characteristics we've labeled ourselves with, we also have very rigid likes, dislikes, preferences, views, opinions and beliefs that we have become very comfortable with. All these serve as our shell, confining us and limiting our potential growth. If you want to break out of your comfort zone, the truth is you will need to physically, mentally and emotionally place yourself in situations that are beyond your comfort. Recognizing areas where you struggle with your ordinary preferences and make an active effort to engage in uncomfortable situations, regardless of how difficult it may be. Most of the time, that feeling of frustration disappears fairly quickly and we see there was nothing to be nervous about. The moment you decide to intentionally enter into an uncomfortable situation, you'll begin to see differences you've made in your life as good.

Step Two: Ignore your first response

Once you recognize a growth opportunity, which comes by a lot more often than you think, your job is to analyze how you automatically react to the situation. What I mean is that we have very habitual responses to situations we perceive as "difficult" or beyond the walls of our comfortable place. If we listened to how we initially responded to situations, we would never change, grow or learn because we would quite literally be stepping on our own feet as we tried to move forward. Who you are now isn't who you have to be for the rest of your life. You are never giving yourself any chance to change if you accept your first response to a difficult situation as "the right one" or "the only one possible."

Step Three: Never stop growing

Life can be a process of perpetual growth, but growth isn't possible without struggling. Find the good in discomfort and let it break the barriers of fear because if you don't, you may never find out who you really are. My favorite example of the growth process is the Butterfly.

The Bible says that this miraculous inside out change is the experience of every true believer! *(Philippians 1:6)* In fact, the very same word used to describe the transformation of a caterpillar into a butterfly is used by the Holy Spirit to describe God's work in us!

The word "miracle" is used to describe the process of a caterpillar's growth (transformation) into a beautiful butterfly. While inside the cocoon, the butterfly is literally being transformed from the inside out. Every part of his inner being is rearranging itself and recreating itself into something new. So even the butterfly experiences the miracle of personal growth. Difference is not bad at all, it's a great step towards a unique you. Mandy Hale said it best, "So you're a little weird? Work it! A little different? Own it! Better to be a nerd than one of the herd!"

Don't be afraid to be weird, don't be afraid to be different, don't worry too much about what other people think. Whatever it is that's original in you and your work might sometimes make you feel uncomfortable. That probably means you're on the right track, so just keep going. Dare to be foolish. ~ Terri Windling

CHAPTER NINE

"Comfortable VS Uncomfortable"

As stated in the previous chapters, "Change doesn't happen by staying in your comfort zone." Period, point blank! If you are serious about creating change, you must embrace your discomfort maturely then choose to go beyond what's commonly expected. Take a look at the feelings of comfort vs discomfort to determine where you are and what you need to do to improve your life results and live a more fulfilled life.

COMFORTABLE: You stop dreaming. You have no visions. You just operate. There was a time when you would explode with excitement about a new idea, but now you have no zeal.

UNCOMFORTABLE: You now feel like you're running out of time and there is much more that you could do! This is a good thing because the urge to do more is what challenges the dreamer in you. Dreaming provokes vision and vision produces success.

COMFORTABLE: You don't have the motivation to work hard for what you want anymore. You do not proceed nor exceed. You just do the bare minimum or nothing at all.

UNCOMFORTABLE: When sitting around idle annoys you and makes you feel useless or you notice a slight annoyance when you spend an entire day doing nothing or less when you should be doing something or more.

COMFORTABLE: You are afraid of change! You stay because at least you know what you are doing where you are. You know what is expected from you with the people in your life and you know what you expect from yourself where you are. You are afraid of new demands and not being able to rise to that occasion.

UNCOMFORTABLE: When what you're holding on to is no longer working. When what you're normally passionate about no longer serves you. When you are now annoyed with the relationships you once enjoyed. When where you are can no longer accommodate who you are.

COMFORTABLE: You complain nonstop and are rude. All of the emotions that you are repressing is coming out in the worst of forms. You mumble complaints, criticize yourself and others, and are pretty rude. You get mad at people with minimal reasons because you are actually expressing your disappointment in yourself for bowing to your fear as opposed to running after your dreams.

UNCOMFORTABLE: When you start having a hard time living by the, "don't sweat the small stuff" motto you are in a uncomfortable place and need to change because nitpicking and always finding something wrong is a hint that there are some underlying issues. The issues can be anything, but it usually indicates an unhappiness with yourself.

COMFORTABLE: You are predictable. People can predict you. You stick to the routine. You are no surprise because everyone even Satan knows your every move; what you are going to do, say, wear, eat, drink and respond.

UNCOMFORTABLE: When being predictable feels like another form of being trapped, but you're alone. Deep down, you hate feeling this way and the thoughts of something more or something bigger stir up the feelings of passion and creativity to do something different.

COMFORTABLE: You have very low expectations for yourself, for the people around you, for the events of your life and for the things that you set out to accomplish. You just go with it because you always know what it might be. Sometimes you want to expect greatness, but you don't.

UNCOMFORTABLE: When the results of low expectations remind you that somehow you've forgotten that you're deserving of the best. When the Feelings of worth flourish and an atmosphere of criticism, discouragement, belittlement, doubt or fear are no longer tolerable. When there is a need to surround yourself with those who have a constructive attitude towards helping you follow your path towards greatness.

COMFORTABLE: You are unbothered by the conditions of your life. Nothing ruffles your feathers, nothing throws you off guard and nothing tees you off. You are just cruising along. You no longer care!

UNCOMFORTABLE: When you are tired of coasting and no longer need permission to rise. When you feel the thorns of life poking you and

Rise up. When you realize that staying where you are is too painful and the pain is provoking you to take the risk.

COMFORTABLE: You are still obsessing over what was. You are immobilized, frozen and focused on perpetual feelings of sadness for all that's gone wrong in life.
UNCOMFORTABLE: When being a victim of the stories you tell yourself is no longer entertaining. When your past pains are now pesky irritations. When you're annoyed by the constant penalty of your past. When holding on to what was becomes more painful than the fear of letting go.

Maturity is recognizing when enough is enough and being okay with not wanting to continue living in the comfortable just because it's familiar. Allow yourself to embrace the discomfort that was meant to provoke you to let go of people, situations, ideas and feelings that aren't conducive to the nourishment of your soul. Go ahead and commit to making choices that nurture your personal growth and give yourself permission to start a new chapter in your life by making the choices that liberate you from following the wrong path and purpose for you. Finally, love yourself enough to choose freedom from anything that hinders you from growing forward.

CHAPTER TEN

"Forgetting & Pressing Is the Key to Progressing"

The life and ministry of the Apostle Paul was dominated by one supreme objective, and it is to this that he refers in Philippians 3:13-14, *"But one thing I do. Forgetting what is behind and press towards what is ahead, I press onward towards the goal which is in Christ Jesus."* Likewise, if we are to succeed in the race of life, we must very deliberately *"forget"* and very deliberately *"press on."* There are a few things which are behind that you should forget if you want to grow toward your destiny that's awaiting. It is not the things we forget that we should have remembered that causes the most trouble. It is the things we remember which we should have forgotten. Strangely enough, a good memory is not always a great asset especially when it hinders your progress! Here are a few things that are ok to forget before you press on.

1. **Forget your past sins.** That is, if you have truly repented, confessed and forsaken them *(Proverbs 28:13)*, then you must forget them. If you have confessed and renounced your sin, God has forgiven it and forgotten it *(1 John 1:9, and compare Psalm 103:12; Isaiah 44:22; Micah 7:19 and Hebrews 10:17)*. If God has forgotten your sins, you must do the same. Otherwise, the memory of them will hinder you.
2. **Forget your past failures.** This is not easy, but if you are constantly dwelling upon your failures and reviving the memory of them, you shall find that your peace is destroyed, your progress is impeded and your usefulness is limited. Some people are always filled with regret over what might have been instead of looking forward to what shall be.
3. **Forget your past successes.** To dwell constantly upon your past achievements will certainly not ensure present victory and it may in fact breed pride. Are you living on a past experience? Are you living on a past reputation?
4. **Forget your past pleasures.** The Children of Israel failed just here, and frequently we read of them crying for the abundance of food and water which they had in Egypt *(Numbers 11:5-6; 20:5 and*

38

21:5) To be engrossed with the past advantages of Egypt is to fail to realize the value of God's present miraculous provision.

5. **Forget your past unhappy experiences**. Has someone let you down? Forget it! To keep reviving the memory of the experience will cause resentment and this will do far more harm to ourselves than to anyone else.

6. **Forget your past blessings.** They are insufficient for today's needs, so we must cry out with the psalmist *(Psalm 103:2)*, but yesterday's provision will not suffice for today's demands. The Lord's provision is "new every morning" *(Lamentations 3:23)*.

7. **Forget the sins and the failures of others.** This needs to be said, for we so easily remember the shortcomings of other people. If you have been wronged, you must forgive and you must forget. Do not say, "I can't!" You can and you must! How? I'm glad you asked. In order to forget, you must reverse the process of remembering. To remember one, must revive the image and keep on reviving it. Now reverse the process; refuse to revive the image. Forget!

Now that you've forgotten, there are things ahead which you must strive to attain. The apostle speaks of three things he reached for which caused him to constantly press.

1. **Press on to perfection.** The first part of verse 12 tells us this, and the word "perfect" means "spiritually mature", not sinless or faultless. The need for growth is implied in Hebrews 6:1; However, in order to grow, you must feed upon the Word of God; you must regularly engage in prayer and stay busy working in the Lord's vineyard.

2. **Press on to take hold of the purpose for which God has taken hold of us.** The second part of verse 12 tells us this. God's general purpose for us is indicated in Romans 8:28-30, but He has a particular purpose for every one of us. Have you discovered God's plan for your life and are you pressing on in it?

3. **Press on with deep concern to win the lost.** This surely should be our attitude. Who could you possibly hinder if you quit? We are in the fourth quarter and the game is almost over which will mean glory for us and gloom for the lost. Let us press on with a

burden to win souls. *(Peter 3:11-12)* What an urgent need there is to come out of your comfort zone!

The ultimate goal of the church (you) is to populate heaven and your ultimate weapon is the gospel of salvation. Satan's ultimate goal is to populate hell and one of his greatest allies for accomplishing this is to keep you comfortable where you are. He knows that you will never change until you get uncomfortable enough to do something different. 2 Cor. 4:3-4 says, *"If our gospel be hid, it is hid to them that are lost: In whom the god of this world hath blinded the minds of them which believe not, lest the light of the glorious gospel of Christ, who is the image of God, should shine unto them."* Your difference is connected to someone's deliverance!

God is looking for men and women who have a heart for Him. He's looking for those who want to take their lives to the next level, step out of the maze of mediocrity and live for something bigger than themselves. *"The fear of man brings a snare, but whoever trusts in and puts his confidence in the Lord will be exalted and safe." (Proverbs 29:25 AMP)*

Father, in the name of Jesus, I ask you for an insatiable desire, one that cannot be satisfied to reach the lost. I ask you for a holy boldness in order to proclaim the truth without hesitancy. Please, Lord, fill my day with divine appointments so that I go from one conversation about your Son to the next. Open doors that man cannot open. I ask you to help me present the gospel message simply and clearly and that you would season my words with grace. Please, Father, give me wisdom in dealing with unbelievers. But most of all, Lord, help me accept my discomfort as an opportunity to change and grow forward so that the lost may see Jesus in me. In Jesus's name, Amen.

THE CONCLUSION

"Prayer & Repentance"

IT'S TIME TO STEP OUT OF YOUR COMFORT ZONE TO ACCEPT JESUS CHRIST AS YOUR LORD AND SAVIOR!

The Bible says, *"For God so loved the world that He gave His one and only Son, [Jesus Christ], that whoever believes in Him shall not perish, but have eternal life"* (John 3:16).

Do you sense God urging you to answer His call to repentance and salvation? I know that stepping out of your comfort zone to accept Jesus Christ as your Lord and Savior may feel like the scariest thing you've ever done, but I am a witness that it's the greatest decision that you'll ever make in life.

So my friend, if you've been sensing that God is calling you to step out of the comfort of your sinful life to accept Jesus as your Lord and Savior and/or to an area of service for Him, I urge and encourage you to say yes to Him today. It is a decision you will never regret and be thankful for all eternity.

Suggested Prayer:

Heavenly Father, thank You that You call each one of us out of darkness and into Your marvelous light. I receive Your forgiveness for all my sins and Your gift of eternal life. Father I desire to serve You with the gifts and talents You have given me. I'm willing to hear and obey Your call to me and ask that You give me the courage to step out of my comfort zone and say yes to you daily. I confess with my mouth and believe in my heart that You died and rose on the third day just for me. Therefore, I choose to make You Lord of my life for the rest of my life. Thank You for hearing and answering my prayer. Gratefully in Jesus's name, Amen.

Congratulations You Are Saved!

STEPS AFTER SALVATION

So you have made your commitment and accepted Jesus Christ as your Lord and Savior. You are ready to "Grow Forward" and live your life for God every day and in every way!

Here are four things that I hope will help you in your new walk with God.

1. Read your Bible every day. This helps you to grow in your faith. It's extremely important that you develop a habit of daily Bible study.

2. Pray. Prayer is simply talking with God. It's important that you pray each day and preferably many times during the day. You can talk to God at any time. It doesn't have to be at a certain time, but it helps to get in the habit of praying each day. For instance set aside a few minutes each morning upon arising to pray to God for that day.

3. Church. Get into a church where Christ is proclaimed. You need to have fellowship with others that are believers. It helps to strengthen you and helps you grow.

4. Witness. Be a witness for Christ by your actions in everyday life. Put a smile on your face when you're at work or school. Go out of your way to help or befriend a person in need and show them Christ's love. Let people know that you are a totally changed person by the way you live your life and by your actions. Living by example is your greatest witness.

Lastly, since you are a new person in Christ, the devil's attacks on your spirit, as well as your faith will probably start to increase. The devil will try to make you doubt that you were ever saved and even try to make you think that all this Christian stuff is not even real. He may even tell you that God isn't listening to you when you pray. 1 Peter 5:8 says, *"Be self-controlled and alert. Your enemy the devil prowls around like a roaring lion looking for someone to devour (NIV)."* Stand strong and firm in your faith and make all the things above a habit and your journey with your wonderful Savior and Lord Jesus Christ will be easier.

REFERENCES

Shaw, George Bernard. (2018, January). "Change Quotes." Retrieved from http://www.Brainy Quotes.com. Famous Quotes. Xplore, Inc.

Allen, Patrick (2018, January). "Get Comfortable being Uncomfortable." Retrieved from https://lifehacker.com/get-comfortable-being-uncomfortable-1599385696

"KJV, NIV, Message & NLT Scriptures." (2018, February) Retrieved from http://www.biblegateway.com/

"The Real Story of An Eagle." (2018, February) Retrieved from http://www.reptilegardens.com/scales-and-tales/article/the-real-story-of-an-eagle

"Butterflies." (2018, March) Retrieved from https://www.encyclopedia.com/plants-and-animals/animals/zoology-invertebrates/butterfly

"Adam Clarke's Commentary." (2018, January) Retrieved from https://www.studylight.org/commentaries/acc/hebrews.html

"Barnes Commentary." (2018, January) Retrieved from https://www.studylight.org/commentaries/wen/hebrews.html

"Merriam-Webster." (2018, March) Retrieved fromhttps://www.merriam-webster.com/dictionary/dictionary

ABOUT THE AUTHOR

Prophet Jessica Selvy-Davis is Co-Pastor and Co-Founder of Kingdom Seekers International Ministry of Arts, where she serves in ministry alongside her husband, Apostle Jonathan Davis. She is a woman who God has graced and gifted with many anointings, and she moves in them fluently and with excellence. She is an Intercessor, Mentor, Praise and Worship Leader, Midwife and a Mother of many.

Prophet Jessica is fueled with a passion to advance God's Kingdom and to make His name praised in the earth. Known for her wit and sense of humor, she ministers effectively to the heart of God's people. She has a tender heart for women. Her desire is for women to break out of the box of limitations and expand their horizon to pursue purpose and destiny. She is valued for her wisdom and intellect, and her integrity is sound. Prophet Jessica governs in the earth realm and is determined to fulfill every prophetic word spoken over her to carry out the spiritual mandate that God has placed in her hands. She is a native of West Memphis, AR, where she serves faithfully for Gods glory.

To request Prophet Jessica Selvy-Davis for speaking engagements, please email:

kingdomseekers_ministryofarts@hotmail.com

To send comments or questions please message her via Email:
lenoraselvy@yahoo.com

Facebook: **www.facebook.com/AuthorJSDavis**

To sow seeds to help further the Gospel of Jesus Christ please send via:
CashApp: **$AuthorJSDavis**
PayPal: **www.paypal.me/AuthorSelvyDavis**

APPENDIX

"I Can Finally See that Where I Am Is Too Small for Me"
Written by Danielle "Qwiet Storm" Glenn

As I sit and I begin to reflect over my life, a thought comes to mind, I was never told being different was a good thing. As a matter of fact I was never taught how to truly embrace my own identity, so I became comfortably uncomfortable with being someone else

Tired of the lies and blinded eyes and that was the point reached in my life when the inner me won the battle not just against what others think or wanted me to be, but against me. I became okay with me taking in all of me which is **U**nique

This **N**ew place felt strange and there were several times when I wanted to complain, but I had a knowing that the sufferings of this present time wouldn't be compared to the glory that would be revealed

Stuck, but in movement, using every gift, every calling creatively created by the creator, I'm committed to the covenant with Christ as I curve chaos **C**onfidently a carrier of God's glory

An outpouring of His spirit like rainfall chosen like the 12 disciples I'm **O**riginal. Even though this **M**ission at times can seem hard, I find myself speaking as Paul, pressing, even with this thorn in my side I declare I'm **F**ocused for there is a prize

The more I wanted to fuss and fight Holy Spirit continually reassured me that my **O**bedience would produce an oil like no other. Yes, you are out of your comfort zone, but you're traveling a journey that is rare following steps that the world would call unfair, but you are a **R**evolutionist and I need your gifts to tangibly show **T**ruth

More **A**lert than ever with an awareness of this place following God as He navigates. Being uncomfortable produced a **B**oldness so great, I find myself beautifully broken in my fathers' face

As I hearken to His voice I Listen for instructions understanding that God is doing a new thing I open myself up for the release. Every lesson imbedded a new strength within me as His everlasting love was uplifting. I can finally see that where I was, was too small for me, but it mended God's will, His purpose and my obedience together and now expansion has hit my life in every area

Now during this journey I've learned to embrace every Experience being the example teaching others how to be comfortable being uncomfortable.